COOKING FOR CATS

For Dixie, with love

COOKING FOR CATS

The healthy, happy way to feed your cat

DEBORA ROBERTSON

PAVILION

First published in the United Kingdom in 2019 by
Pavilion
An imprint of HarperCollinsPublishers
1 London Bridge Street
London SE1 9GF

www.harpercollins.co.uk

HarperCollinsPublishers
1st Floor, Watermarque Building, Ringsend Road
Dublin 4, Ireland

ISBN 978-1-911624-67-7

A CIP catalogue record for this book is available from the British Library.

10 9 8 7 6 5 4 3 2
Reproduction by Mission Productions Ltd
Printed and bound in China

www.pavilionbooks.com

MIX
Paper | Supporting
responsible forestry
FSC™ C007454

*Cooking
for Cats*

CONTENTS

How It Began

When my husband Séan and I acquired our first cats, Delphi and Liberty, twenty years ago, we did what we thought we were supposed to do. We began feeding them a high-quality dry food with suitably scientific-looking packaging. Every morning and every evening, we dutifully doled out the specified amounts using the scoop provided. So far, so joyless. They would sniff it with their beautiful noses, sometimes pat it with their dainty velvet paws. And then they might wander off, coming back to it later, maybe, sometime. See ya! Trees to climb, sofas to shred, more exciting stuff to do.

I can't say my feelings weren't hurt. I write recipes for humans for a living. I am used to people diving into my culinary offerings with glee. But here they were, these two snooty Burmese princesses, turning their noses up at the meals I was serving them. And who can blame them? Dried kibble. Every day. Wouldn't you be a little put out? I know I would.

I began to feed them commercial wet food. This was an improvement – at least they looked happy to see me when I ventured into the kitchen, swirling around my ankles, rubbing their soft and eager little bodies against my calves in a hungry dance of pleasure. They would dive into their food, eating everything and clattering their bowls halfway across the floor as they licked every remaining morsel.

Then, because I can't help myself, I began cooking for them too. If you come into my house, I am going to make you something to eat. Them's the rules. It made me – and them – inordinately happy. I've rarely had such an enthusiastic response from my human friends to elaborate marinated, seasoned, garnished and otherwise primped-up dishes than I had from Delphi and Liberty to some simply poached chicken or steamed fish.

But cats can be a challenge. Unlike dogs, who are invariably ruled by their stomachs, cats can be fussy (or discerning, see page 23). They might like something to eat, or to chase a leaf with laser-focused concentration, or to bask in a puddle of sunshine on a chair by the window.

I am reminded of this daily when I look at my two dogs, Gracie and Barney, wolfing down their food, so much so that Gracie has to have a special bowl with a sort of maze in the bottom to stop her from guzzling her dinner without drawing a single breath. Meanwhile, Dixie, the elegant Burmese who currently deigns to live with us, eats with enormous grace and discernment. For her, elegance is refusal. And of course, I feel crestfallen if she rejects my offerings at mealtimes, but I have learned what she likes, and that's a mixture of really good, complete, canned food, some of my special dinners, and the occasional homemade treat. Give the lady what she wants, I say. She is sleek and healthy and has the energy and spirit of a tiny tiger.

I am sharing with you here some of the favourite dishes and treats I have created for the five cats we have loved over the past two decades. And, because cats deserve all good things, I've included some simple craft projects too, to help them feel loved, happy and entertained. Sharing our home with our cats has given me so much pleasure over the years, so these offerings feel like a very small gesture of thanks for all their boundless affection. I hope your cats will enjoy them too.

'In ancient times, cats were worshipped as gods. They have not forgotten this.'

Terry Pratchett

Chapter One

THE CAT'S LARDER

My cat Dixie is quite the connoisseur.
She has her likes and dislikes - in fact, she is far
more discerning than most of my human friends,
and certainly more so than her canine brother and
sister, Barney and Gracie. In this chapter, I'm sharing
all the things I have on hand to keep her happy.
It will arm you with all the information you need
to start cooking for your own cat, whether she is
a fussy feline or an enthusiastic glutton.

WHAT TO EAT?

In the wild, cats are carnivores. They hunt and eat what they catch, and very few of their nutritional needs are met by eating plants. With my own cat, Dixie, I try to keep her diet as close as possible to the kinds of foods she might eat in the wild. I feed her a combination of fresh foods I make myself and commercial food with as short an ingredient list as possible. I go big on rabbit, chicken, duck and lamb, with the occasional bit of poached or canned fish or steamed prawns (shrimp). I keep the meat content of her diet as close to 90 per cent of what she eats as I can. And yes, I do give her the occasional treat, for training, bonding and as an expression of my boundless love for her dear, sweet, aristocratic self.

The reason I don't cook all of Dixie's food is that developing a complete feline diet is a very complex thing. To get it completely right involves grinding up bones and an animal dietician's knowledge of which supplements might be required. I am not that person. If you think you might be, buy a good-quality meat grinder and seek professional advice. I feed my cat home-cooked food about 30 per cent of the time, with a high-quality commercial wet food such as Lily's Kitchen or Nature's Menu (see Resources, page 108), which are grain free and very low in carbs, making up the balance of her food.

'Dogs eat. Cats dine.'

Ann Taylor

Unlike dogs, cats can't effectively digest a wide range of grains, fruits and vegetables. This is why, in theory, dogs can exist on a vegetarian diet and cats can't. Cats need taurine and arginine, amino acids found exclusively in meat, and their absence can lead to heart problems, tooth decay and blindness. Therefore, it is absolutely vital to feed them food with a very high meat content.

In a lot of commercial cat food, cheap, carby fillers such as corn, wheat and rice are used in abundance. Make sure you examine the labels on the commercial foods you feed your cat. Cheaper foods often have very poor nutritional value and can lead to painful (and expensive) health problems further down the line. Look for something with a high meat content where the carbs come from vegetables and healthier grains such as millet, which is less likely to trigger allergic reactions (see Dealing with Allergies and Intolerances, page 103). It is important, too, that the food you choose is suitable for your cat's life stage, from kitten, to adult (1-6 years), to senior (7 years and over).

IS MY CAT FAT?

Overfeeding is a much more significant problem for cats than underfeeding. While we all might love a cuddly cat (Bagpuss Syndrome), we really are killing them with misguided kindness. Carrying too much weight - as with humans - can lead to quite serious health problems, from diabetes to cardiovascular disease, liver problems, arthritis and urinary tract disease, and there's nothing cute about that. It's quite sobering to think that around a third of Britain's cats are technically obese.

To judge whether or not your cat is overweight, stand above her and look down. She should go in at the waist and when you look at her from the side, her belly shouldn't sag. You should be able to feel her ribs, but not see them. If you are worried she is overweight - or underweight - check with your vet that there are no other underlying health problems and discuss what you can do to help your cat to return to slinky top form.

To help your cat to lose weight, start by cutting down on her food by between 10 and 15 per cent - much more than that can lead to liver problems. Cats have a very specific metabolic reaction to fasting or a rapid, dramatic reduction in their food intake, and a diet that is too heavily and quickly restricted can lead to hepatic lipidosis, or fatty liver disease.

You should also try to increase her activity levels. I appreciate this isn't quite so simple as it is with dogs, and it will require you to be a little more ingenious. However, even the laziest of cats can usually be lured into a little light exercise with the help of a length of ribbon, some puzzle toys containing the occasional, difficult-to-get-at treat, fishing-pole toys (see page 30) and perhaps a laser pointer (remember never to point this directly into anyone's eyes, feline or human). If your cat is an indoor cat, it's even more important to try to increase her activity as much as you can (and it will probably do you some good, too – after a difficult day, playing with Dixie and seeing the world through her eyes for a few minutes is one of the greatest stress-relievers I know).

HOW MANY TIMES A DAY SHOULD I FEED MY CAT?

Kittens with tiny tummies need three or four small meals each day, whereas adult cats are fine with being fed once or twice a day. With my cat Dixie, I prefer to feed her twice a day as I don't like leaving out a lot of fresh food at a time (see Why Free Feeding is Not a Good Idea, page 18), and also because mealtimes are such a good opportunity to bond with your cat. I don't think I am ever more popular than when I am laying down a bowl of rabbit stew (see page 52).

WHY FREE FEEDING IS NOT A GOOD IDEA

Shortly after we got married, my husband and I got our first kittens, Delphi and Liberty. We took them to their first check-up and our vet, Russell, gave us advice I have lived by ever since. He said, 'They're bonsai tigers and you should treat them as such, don't forget about their essential nature in the wild.'

In the wild, cats hunt, then eat, then rest, then repeat. Their stomachs have not evolved to graze constantly through the day, but to eat and then fast - even if it's only for a few hours. Free-grazing cats are more likely to be fat. Russell told us to replicate their natural eating pattern by putting down their food, giving them time to eat it, but then picking up anything they leave. Of course, this is particularly important if you are feeding them fresh food which might spoil and develop harmful bacteria, especially on hot days. Even if you are feeding them dry food, you should still remove their bowls after mealtimes. Whatever you are feeding them, it is absolutely vital that they have access to fresh water at all times.

WET OR DRY?

The appeal of dry, complete cat food is that it's convenient and long-lasting, and for many years, vets encouraged their clients to serve dry food because it was thought to be better for cats' teeth, although more recent research on this is inconclusive.

Generally speaking, cats find wet food more enticing and will eat it in one go (if they don't, it's possible you are leaving out too much food). It also has a higher water content - closer to the 70 per cent or so they would consume in their wild diets. This is significant because too dry a diet can lead to them forming crystals or stones in their urine, which can be terribly painful and harmful. Wet food is also more appealing to kittens, and to older cats who may have less-than-perfect teeth and gums.

A WHOLE LOT OF LITTER

A lot of what goes in must come out. Picking the right litter and litter tray is essential to making your cat feel truly at home. Would you be inclined to use a filthy bathroom or a clean one? Your cat is just the same. If the litter tray is not to her liking, she may be more inclined to take care of her business in your neighbours' gardens - never conducive to happy neighbourhood relations - or, worse, around the house.

I have always bought my cats litter trays that have lids on them, to stop them kicking litter all over the place, and for their privacy, which is so important to cats. If you're using an open one, make sure it's sited in a place where they feel safe and secure, and also try to place it as far away as possible from their food and water bowls. I have two trays for Dixie, one on the ground floor and one upstairs. Generally, it's advisable to have one tray per cat in a multi-cat household, plus one extra.

When it comes to choosing litter, it can often be a question of trial and error to discover the one they like the best. I like a clumping one which also has an odour-control element. It's very important to keep the tray clean, removing dirty litter very frequently, at least once a day. When I clean Dixie's tray, I just use dishwashing liquid and very hot water - some sanitizing products, such as Dettol, are toxic to cats so check before you use them.

POO!

Cats are nature's stoics. They are very good at disguising when they feel unwell, so we owners have to become finely attuned to any signs that they are not on top form. So – well – it pays to pay attention to their poo. When you are cleaning the litter tray, what you should see are poos that are dark brown and firm, a bit like clay, which hold their shape. If the poo is black instead of dark brown, it may indicate that your cat are also passing blood; if it's very pale, it might indicate liver disease. In both cases, you should call your vet. If the poos are small and hard, it means she constipated – try to encourage her to drink more water by putting down more bowls around your home and add some moist foods, such as puréed squash, to her diet. If her poos are watery, it might indicate allergies, parasites or bacterial infection. If any of these symptoms persist for longer than a couple of days, you know the drill: call your vet.

Raw feeding

In recent years, more and more people have become interested in feeding their cats and dogs on raw diets, sometimes called the BARF diet (bones and raw food). Cats don't need carbs or vegetables, though they will tolerate them in small quantities, and the ones I've included in this book are there really to add variety to their food and increase their pleasure in eating it. Those who advocate a raw diet argue that it is as close as possible to their diet in nature and while some are almost evangelical about the benefits, there are things to consider before you try it. Cooking meat destroys nasties such as the protozoan parasite that causes toxoplasmosis, as well as bacteria such as salmonella and listeria, which can be very harmful, even deadly. It is also not the simplest exercise to ensure your cat has a balanced raw diet and you should certainly consult your vet before you give it a try, and ask them to refer you to an animal nutritionist.

There are commercial companies that sell balanced, raw food which is already ground up and easy for your cat to digest. I have given Dixie both Nature's Menu and Natural Instinct (see Resources, page 108). They're complete cat foods and she did quite well on them, though I confess she seems to prefer cooked food when she has the choice.

How interested are cats in variety?

Cats are biologically programmed to kill and eat fresh meat. They are not scavengers, unless in desperate circumstances, as they have heightened senses of taste and smell which prevent them from eating spoiled food. What we sometimes interpret as fussiness is really an enhanced awareness, which has helped to keep them safe. Unlike my dogs, who will eat all manner of extraordinary things, Dixie does not cause me concern as she is so cautious, although I do, of course, keep an eye on her. Most cats are conservative eaters. They may not need or want loads of variety, which is why it feels so rewarding to introduce them to new flavours they love.

23

'There are no ordinary cats.'

Colette

Can cats be vegetarians?

Cats are obligate carnivores, which is to say that unlike dogs, they have evolved to eat a diet which comprises almost exclusively meat. Their bodies are efficient eating machines, designed to digest small prey - flesh, bones, organs and all. To maintain perfect health, they require specific amino acids (the building blocks of protein) such as taurine and arginine (see What to Eat, page 14), essential fatty acids and vitamins which are found in meat. Without these, they will become seriously ill and their lives will certainly be shortened. They can enjoy small amounts of fruit and vegetables for variety, as you will see in the recipes in this book, but the majority of their nutrition should come from hearty, meaty meals.

Top Tips

GOOD THINGS

Fish

Fish is not a natural food for cats. They are desert animals, remember? But a little fish from time to time is fine. Poached or steamed white fish or salmon is usually popular. You might sometimes want to feed them canned fish - sardines and mackerel are a good source of Omega 3 fatty acids and as they're so smelly, they can be a good way of concealing pills or other medication your cat requires. If you think your cat might be constipated or plagued by a hairball, a very small amount of fish oil from the can may help. All cats seem to adore tuna, but it should be fed very sparingly (see The Tuna Conundrum, page 66).

Eggs

Cats should not eat raw eggs, but a small amount of cooked egg from time to time is a good source of protein and amino acids.

Fruit

Cats tend not to be crazy about fruit as they lack flavour receptors for sweetness. Small amounts of fruit from time to time can help aid digestion though, particularly if they are constipated. Peeled and cored pieces of apple, small bites of banana, and blueberries – which most cats also love to chase across the floor – are good choices.

Vegetables

Vegetables such as broccoli, sweet potatoes, peas, spinach, green beans and squash, lightly cooked and cut up into small pieces, are a good source of fibre, but ensure they don't make up more than 10 per cent of your cat's diet.

Meat and game

About 90 per cent of your cat's diet should be made up of lean meat. Make sure you cut off any excess fat as it can cause pancreatitis, which is extremely painful and can be fatal. Poultry, rabbit and lamb are very good sources of protein; while some cats like beef too, it is the most allergenic meat (See Dealing with Allergies and Intolerances, page 103).

Liver and other organ meats

These are very rich sources of protein, vitamins and minerals and most cats find them delicious. They also usually have the benefit of being relatively inexpensive.

Top Tips
BAD THINGS

Chocolate

Chocolate contains theobromine and if cats ingest it, it can be fatal. In most cases, the darker the chocolate (i.e. the higher the cocoa content), the more toxic it is.

Alcohol and caffeinated drinks

Of course, I realize you're not sitting down with your cat for a cocktail or a coffee, but they are curious creatures and may sometimes sip something you leave lying around on the table or floor, so be vigilant.

Dog food

Though dog food is not toxic to cats, your cat needs a very different set of nutrients. Cat food should contain plenty of vitamin A, taurine, arachidonic acid and protein, while dog food has much lower levels of these nutrients as their need for vitamin A and protein is less. They are also able to produce taurine and arachidonic acid, but cats must obtain these acids from their food. Without a sufficient amount of taurine, cats can develop heart disease or vision and dental issues.

Onions and garlic

If eaten by cats, onions, garlic, leeks, shallots and spring onions (scallions) – in fact all members of the allium family – can damage red blood cells and lead to anaemia.

Dairy

While cats might enjoy milk, cream and cheese, they have trouble digesting lactose and it can cause upset stomachs and diarrhoea. A small amount of unsweetened, plain live yogurt is an acceptable occasional treat though.

Grapes and raisins

Ingesting even a small amount of grapes or raisins can cause kidney failure in cats. Some cats may show no symptoms before becoming very ill indeed, so be vigilant – it's best not to keep them in the fruit bowl, and pick up any that you may drop on the floor before 'chase the toxic fruit' becomes a potentially dangerous game.

HOW TO MAKE A
FISHING
POLE TOY

I've never met a cat who didn't love a fishing pole toy. Chase and
pounce is the bump and grind of the cat world. You want a pole long
enough so they don't accidentally pounce on your fingers with their
claws out (I speak from experience). I paint the pole, but obviously
your cat couldn't care less whether it's painted or not. The paint is for
you, so do skip that stage if you want, although if you're going to give
it as a present to a cat-owning friend it does make for a prettier gift.

> *'Time spent with cats is never wasted.'*

May Sarton

- 1 piece of dowel, approximately 50-60cm/20-24in long
- Some non-toxic paint – I like Nutshell Natural Paints (see Resources, page 108), a sample pot will do
- Paintbrush
- Pet-safe glue – I like Gorilla wood glue
- 50-60cm/20-24in rope, 6mm/¼in thick – you can use the 6mm/¼in cat rope from Ropelocker (see Resources, page 108) if you like, or just use string, although it may not last as long
- Some scraps of felt
- Needle and thread
- Approx 20-30cm/8-12in thin ribbon

1. Paint the dowel and leave to dry.

2. Cover 10cm/4in of one end of the dowel with glue. Beginning from the end of the glued area, wind the rope tightly around the dowel until you reach the end of it. Press firmly to ensure it is all attached. Dab a tiny amount of glue at the stuck-down end of the rope to stop it from fraying. Leave to dry.

3. Cut 3-5 fish shapes of various sizes from the felt. At the point where the fishs' tails begin to fork, or at the end of their noses, use a needle and thread to stitch them to the rope, about 2cm/¾in from the end of it. Bind the ribbon around the fish at the point where you sewed them on, winding it round several times before sealing it with a tight knot – this helps to conceal the stitches, but if you leave the ends of the ribbon dangling, it adds extra chase-and-pounce interest for your cat.

 Tip You can also add pompoms and bells to your fishing pole toy if you like.

Chapter Two

EVERYDAY TREATING

This chapter contains some simple, everyday meals and treats you can use to introduce a little variety into your cat's diet. From easy omelettes to turkey meatballs, fishcakes and chicken soup, it gives inspiration for ways to tempt even the most refined sophisti-cats. Extra bonuses are that you can make most of these dishes with items you probably already have in your refrigerator or larder and they are almost embarrassingly uncomplicated to prepare.

MIAOUSLI YOGURT BREAKFAST

- 🐾 ½ small apple, peeled, cored and chopped into small dice, or grated
- 🐾 ½ small banana, finely chopped
- 🐾 1 tbsp plain yogurt
- 🐾 1 tsp rolled oats (oatmeal)

Makes
1–2
servings

Although dairy is unsuitable for most cats (see page 29), a little yogurt from time to time can be beneficial because of its probiotic properties, particularly if your cat is suffering from constipation. It is very important that the yogurt doesn't contain any artificial sweeteners or flavourings.

1.   Mix everything together in a bowl. Serve immediately.

2.   If this portion is too large for your cat, divide it up and enjoy the rest yourself, perhaps with a trickle of honey.

DID YOU KNOW?

Cats produce around 100 different sounds, but they use meowing almost exclusively to communicate with humans. They seldom meow to each other, probably because their mothers stopped responding once they were weaned.

SARDINE OMELETTE

Cooked eggs make a tasty occasional treat and they're a good source of protein. Sardines can tempt the trickiest of palates – just be sure to blot off any excess oil before mashing.

- 🐾 1 sardine, canned in olive oil with no added salt, plus 1 tsp oil from the can
- 🐾 2 eggs, lightly beaten
- 🐾 1 tsp finely chopped fresh parsley (optional)

Makes
1
omelette

1. Blot the sardine with kitchen paper to remove excess oil. In a small bowl, mash it finely with a fork, then stir in the parsley if using.

2. Tip 1 tsp olive oil from the sardine can into a small non-stick frying pan (skillet). Rub it across the surface using kitchen paper so you leave the barest trace on the pan. Warm over a medium-high heat, then pour in the beaten eggs and use a spatula to lift up the edges, swirling the pan so the uncooked egg runs to the sides.

3. When the egg is cooked through (it needs to be drier than it would be if making an omelette for humans, as raw egg is bad for cats), tip it onto a plate and spread the sardine mixture over the top.

4. Once the omelette is cool enough to handle, roll it up tightly and cut it into thin slices of about 1.5cm/^{5}/$_8$ in. Any omelette your cat doesn't eat can be frozen for up to 3 months.

VARIATIONS

In place of the sardine, you can use a couple of tablespoons of puréed squash, mashed sweet potato, chopped cooked prawns (shrimp) or shredded cooked chicken. Use a small amount of olive oil to lightly grease the pan.

CHICKEN SOUP

This is a favourite in our house and I make it in vast quantities, then freeze in batches. Sometimes I strain off the broth to make a more solid meal (save some to pour over drier dinners) or to tempt a cat who is off his food. If you think your cat is dehydrated, it is often easier to encourage him to drink a slightly warmed broth than water.

- 4 skinless chicken breasts
- 1 carrot, peeled and roughly chopped
- 1 celery stalk, trimmed and roughly chopped
- 2 litres/3½ pints/2 quarts water
- A selection of vegetables chopped small, such as sweet potato, courgettes (zucchini), squash, green beans and/or broccoli – a couple of handfuls

1. Place the chicken in a saucepan with the carrot and celery. Add the water. Bring to a simmer and skim off any foam which rises to the top. Cook gently for about 40 minutes, until the chicken is very tender. Strain the stock into a clean saucepan.

2. When the chicken is cool, shred it into very small pieces. Return it to the pan with the stock, along with the cooked carrot and celery and any raw vegetables from the list. Simmer for about 15 minutes, or until all the vegetables are very tender.

3. This will keep, covered, in the refrigerator for a couple of days or freeze it in individual portions for up to 4 months.

TURKEY AND SQUASH MEATBALLS

Squash is a good source of fibre and is tolerated by most cats, especially when combined with turkey which they all seem to love. You can use chicken in this recipe if you prefer.

- 150g/5½oz/1¼ cups peeled, deseeded squash, cut into 2-cm/¾-in cubes
- 500g/1lb 2oz/2 cups minced (ground) turkey or chicken
- 1 tsp finely chopped fresh mint

1. Preheat the oven to 200°C/Fan 180°C/400°F/ Gas 6. Line a roasting pan with parchment paper.

2. Using a steamer or sieve (strainer) set over a pan of boiling water, steam the squash until it is very soft. Transfer to a bowl and mash it roughly. Leave to steam for about 10 minutes, so it loses some of its moisture. When it has cooled, mix in the turkey or chicken and the mint until everything is well combined.

3. Roll into walnut-sized meatballs and place in the prepared pan. Bake in the preheated oven for 25 minutes until cooked through and very lightly browned. Cool before feeding to your cat.

4. The meatballs will keep in the refrigerator for a couple of days or you can freeze them for up to 4 months.

Makes
30
approx.

SALMON
FISH CAKES

🐾 1 x 200-g/7-oz can of salmon with no added salt, drained, or 200g/7oz/1 cup cooked salmon, finely flaked

🐾 40g/1½oz/scant ½ cup cucumber, grated

🐾 50g/2oz/¼ cup cooked millet (cooked weight)

🐾 1 tbsp finely chopped fresh parsley

🐾 ¼ tsp Plaque Off (optional, see Resources, page 108)

Makes
2-3
fishcakes

This is a simple and quick recipe, which I can usually make from what I have in the store cupboard. If you think it's a faff to cook such a small serving of millet, you'd be right. Cook a decent amount and fluff the remaining grains (technically a seed, fact fans) into a salad for yourself, or freeze it in ice-cube trays for later.

•·•·••·•·•·••·••·••·•••••••·••·••·•••••••·

1. To cook millet, place one part millet to two parts water in a pan, bring to the boil, then reduce to a simmer and cook for 25 minutes, stirring from time to time (or follow the instructions on the packet). Freeze it in ice-cube trays and then, once frozen, decant into a freezer bag to store, so you always have serving-size portions on hand.

2. In a bowl, mix everything together until well combined. Form into two or three patties, depending on the size of your cat. Serve one patty as a meal and store the rest, covered, in the refrigerator for up to 2 days, or in the freezer for up to 4 months.

SCRAMBLED EGGS WITH CHICKEN LIVERS

This is an easy and nutritious meal. I sometimes give it to Dixie when she is feeling a little under the weather and she wolfs - or lions - it right down.

- 🐾 ¼tsp olive oil
- 🐾 2 eggs, lightly beaten
- 🐾 40-50g/1½-2oz chicken livers, cleaned and trimmed of sinews
- 🐾 Pinch of Plaque Off, optional (see Resources, page 108)

Makes
1-2
servings

1. Warm the oil in a small non-stick pan over a medium-low heat.
    Add the eggs and cook, stirring, until they form soft curds.
    Of course, you can do this in a microwave, if you prefer.
    Scoop them into a bowl to cool while you cook
    the livers.

2. Tip the livers into the same pan in which you cooked the eggs
    with a splash of water and cook over a medium-high heat
    until they are cooked through with no hint of pink in the
    centre. This shouldn't take more than 4-5 minutes. Stir
    into the eggs.

3. Once the livers are cool, spoon some into a bowl for your
    cat – how big a serving depends on the size of your cat
    and how hungry she is. Sprinkle on some Plaque Off if you
    are using it. Any leftovers can be kept, covered, in the
    refrigerator for a day.

Where to feed your cat

If cats are stressed or anxious, they often avoid their food. Once or twice a year, we take Dixie on the five-hour drive to my parents' house and often she doesn't eat much the following day, but it doesn't have to be anything quite so dramatic as that to put them off their food. It could be disruption within your own household, such as visitors your cat isn't quite sure about, noisy kids running about, or almost anything that disrupts her calm routine. Try to put your cat's bowls in a spot where she can have some privacy and peace, away from your home's main thoroughfares. Also try to place them away from any windows – if you live in an area with a lot of local cats, yours may be hypervigilant to those crossing her territory while she is trying to eat. A cosy, quiet corner would be perfect.

KEEP IT CLEAN

It is very important to make sure your cat's bowls are scrupulously clean. They will often reject food from a less-than-pristine bowl – well, wouldn't you? Wash bowls in hot soapy water after every use. And make sure you rinse them well, as cats' heightened sense of smell means that they may reject the food if they can still smell the dishwashing detergent on the bowl.

HOW TO MAKE A
SCRATCHING
POST

Cats love to scratch. They do it to stretch their bodies and clean and sharpen their claws. It's their yoga. If you wish to deter them from practising one of their favourite activities on your family heirloom sofa or precious carpets, make a scratching post. Or several scratching posts – in this case, more is better. For sisal rope, I like buying from Ropelocker (see Resources, page 108) – they sell untreated 6-mm/ $1/4$ -in sisal specifically designed for pet toys.

- Non-toxic paint – I like Nutshell Natural Paints (see Resources, page 108)
- Paintbrush
- A piece of MDF (medium density fibreboard) or heavy wood for the base, approx 70 x 70cm/28 x 28 in
- 10 x 10-cm/4 x 4-in piece of wood, at least 60cm/24in long – a fence post will do
- Post cap, for the top of the wood
- Pencil
- Drill
- 4 x 5-cm/2-in wood screws
- Screwdriver
- Sisal rope, about 30-50m/32-54 yards, depending how long your post is (see above)
- Staples and staple gun
- Pet-safe glue – I like Gorilla wood glue
- Some ribbon and bells or other small cat toys (optional)

1. Paint the base, the fence post and cap and leave to dry completely. Add a second coat to the base and cap if you think it is required (the post will be covered by the rope).

2. Centre the post on the base and draw around it with a soft pencil. Drill four guideholes about 1cm/ $1/2$ in diagonally in from the corners of the square. Place the base on one end of the post and, from the underside of the base, screw the two together.

Cont'd ❧

3. Staple the end of the sisal firmly into the base of the post. Working about 10cm/4in at a time, spread glue over the post and begin wrapping the rope around the post and sticking it down, making sure you keep it close together and tightly wrapped. Leave it to dry completely.

4. If you're using them, tie the bells or small cat toys (I use the catnip mice, see page 70, or fish cut out of felt) to lengths of ribbon and staple them into the top of the post. Use the wood glue to stick the post cap to the top of the scratching post.

5. Take a bow.

 Tips

🐾 If you have any leftover carpet, you can glue that onto the base instead of painting it.

🐾 A sturdy tree branch with its bark intact works really well in place of the fence post and looks great. Wrap the sisal around part of it and leave the rest bare.

🐾 Instead of finishing the scratching post with the post cap, you could attach a small platform for your cat to sit on.

🐾 If you can't be bothered with all the faff, simply buy a traffic cone. They're very cheap to buy from building supply stores. (Don't steal one. You are not a student.) Glue the sisal rope onto that.

'What greater gift than the
love of a cat?'

Charles Dickens

Chapter Three

ONE-POT DISHES

The appeal of one-pot cooking for your cat is the same as one-pot cooking for your human family. It's easy, inexpensive and nutritious, and with one burst of effort, you can create freezable meals which will save you time in the long run. Don't get too hung up on having every ingredient in each recipe. If you don't have beef, substitute chicken. No sweet potato? Add broccoli. No parsley? Leave it out - your cat won't mind.

RABBIT STEW

Rabbit is a very healthy, lean meat and is often available from good butchers and even some supermarkets now – it's relatively inexpensive, too. If you see it and you have room in your freezer, stock up and you'll have the building blocks for many happy kitty dinners.

- 🐾 1 tsp olive oil
- 🐾 1 or 2 rabbits, jointed (a prepared rabbit should weigh 600–800g/1lb 5oz–1lb 12oz)
- 🐾 750ml/26fl oz/3¼ cups vegetable or chicken stock (if using a store-bought one, make sure it has no added salt) or simply use water
- 🐾 200g/7oz/1½ cups green beans, topped and tailed and cut into 1-cm/½-in pieces
- 🐾 1 carrot, cut into 1-cm/½-in dice
- 🐾 1 celery stalk, cut into 1-cm/½-in dice
- 🐾 1 sweet potato, cut into 1-cm/½-in dice
- 🐾 4 tsbp finely chopped fresh parsley

Makes
1
large pot

1.   Warm the olive oil in a large casserole dish over a medium-high heat. Add the rabbit pieces and sauté until just browned. Add the stock or water - you need enough to cover the rabbit, so top up the stock with water if you don't have enough. Bring to a simmer, then cover and simmer very gently for about 1¼ hours or until the meat is really tender. Check for tenderness, as some rabbits are tougher than others.

2.   Add the chopped vegetables and cook for a further 15 minutes.

3.   Cool, and when the meat is comfortable to handle, remove and shred it, pulling every scrap from the bones. Be careful to ensure there are no bones left in the stew, as rabbit bones can be very sharp.

4.   Return the meat to the stew and stir in the parsley. It will keep sealed in the refrigerator for 3-4 days, or in the freezer for up to 4 months.

BONE BROTH

You need as large a pan as you can get your hands on to make this bone broth – there should be plenty of water circulating around the bones. Obviously this is simply a beefed up stock, simmered for hours and hours to extract every scrap of goodness; the vinegar helps to extract all of the minerals from the bones. You need to simmer everything together for longer than you can possibly imagine – I do it for at least 12 hours – so pick a day when you're pottering around the house so you can keep an eye on it.

- 🐾 2–3kg/4½–6¾lb beef bones and/or lamb bones
- 🐾 2 carrots, scrubbed and roughly chopped
- 🐾 2 celery stalks, roughly chopped
- 🐾 2 tbsp cider vinegar

Makes
1
large pot

1. Place all of the ingredients in a large stockpot and pour in enough water to cover the bones by about 5cm/2in. Bring to the boil, skim off any scum which rises to the surface, then partially cover with a lid and simmer very, very gently – you want the barest of bubbles to rise to the surface – for a minimum of 12 hours, up to 24 hours if you want a good, jellied set (see Variation). Keep an eye on the pan and give it all a good stir every few hours to make sure nothing is sticking. You may need to add a little boiling water from the kettle from time to time if the liquid level looks low.

2. When you have finished simmering the broth, place a fine sieve (strainer) over a large bowl or pan and strain the broth into it. If the pan is too heavy (it probably will be), start the process by scooping the broth from the pan with a jug (pitcher) or ladle until the pan is light enough to lift.

3. Sealed in a container, the stock will keep in the refrigerator for up to 5 days, or in the freezer for 4 months. I like to freeze it in ice cube trays so I can defrost small amounts quickly when I need them.

VARIATION

If I have leftover scraps of roast meat, I sometimes set them in a little broth which I have simmered for long enough that it forms a jelly. This might be Dixie's favourite meal on earth.

SPRING CHICKEN CASSEROLE

I always cook chicken or other meats on the bone if I can, as there are a lot of beneficial nutrients in the bones. It is very important, however, that when you shred the meat you don't leave a scrap of bone behind – cooked bones are very brittle and can cause choking. If you have some chicken livers, adding them to this casserole gives a great nutritional boost. Just drop them in at the same time as you add the vegetables.

🐾 4 chicken legs, about 1kg/2lb 4oz, skinned

🐾 100g/3½oz/¾ cup peas (frozen peas are fine)

🐾 1 courgette (zucchini), cut into 1-cm/½-in dice

🐾 1 small head of broccoli, stem trimmed, chopped very small (chop the stem too, if it's not too woody)

Makes
1
large pot

1. Put the chicken into a large saucepan and pour over just enough water to cover. Bring to the boil and skim off any scum that rises to the top. Lower the heat to a bare simmer, cover and poach for about 30 minutes until the chicken is very tender.

2. Remove the chicken from the stock to cool (retain the stock), then shred the chicken from the bones and cut it very small. Return the meat to the pan with the stock and the vegetables, bring to the boil and simmer for 15 minutes. If there is too much liquid, strain some off and freeze it (see page 65) to use in other recipes.

3. The casserole will keep sealed in the refrigerator for 3-4 days, or in the freezer for up to 4 months.

BEEF AND
BROWN RICE DINNER

Some brown rice from time to time adds fibre to your cat's diet
and aids his digestive system.

- 600g/1lb 5oz diced beef, such as stewing steak, 5% fat
- 80g/3oz/¹/₂ cup brown rice, rinsed
- 550ml/19fl oz/2¹/₃ cups water
- 100g/3¹/₂oz/³/₄ cup green beans, topped and tailed and
  cut into 1-cm/¹/₂-in lengths

Makes
1
large pot

1. Put the beef, rice and water into a large saucepan and bring to the boil. Give everything a stir, turn down the heat, cover with a lid and simmer for about 30 minutes until the rice is almost cooked.

2. Add the green beans and cook for a further 5 minutes (add more boiling water from the kettle if you need to), until the rice is fully cooked and the beans are soft. Remove from the heat and let the pan sit for a further 5-10 minutes with the lid on so the rice can absorb more of the liquid (although it doesn't really matter if it is a bit soupy).

3. This will keep sealed in the refrigerator for a day or so, or in the freezer for up to 4 months.

LAMB AND DILL HOTPOT

- 1kg/2lb 4oz diced, boneless leg of lamb or lamb shoulder
- 100g/3½oz peeled and deseeded butternut squash, or 100g/3½oz/ ¾ cup sweet potato, and cut into 1-cm/½-in dice
- 1 carrot, cut into 1-cm/½-in dice
- 1 celery stalk, cut into 1-cm/½-in dice
- 1 tbsp chopped fresh dill

Makes
1
large pot

My cat Dixie loves this dish. I add dill here for its alleged mild calming properties, though I can't really say it deters her from running up the curtains that much.

• •

1. Put the lamb into a saucepan and pour over enough water to cover. Bring to the boil and skim off any scum that rises to the top. Lower the heat to a bare simmer, cover and poach for about 1 hour until the lamb is very tender.

2. Add the vegetables, bring to the boil and simmer for 15 minutes until the vegetables are very soft. Stir in the dill. Cool completely and skim fat off the top. You can purée some or all of this hotpot if it makes it more appealing to your cat.

3. This will keep sealed in the refrigerator for 3-4 days, or in the freezer for up to 4 months.

FISH SUPPER

You can use any firm white fish in this dish instead of salmon, if you prefer. Grating and shredding the vegetables makes them easy for cats to eat and also means that you can cook this dish in next to no time.

- 🐾 400ml/14fl oz/1³/₄ cups water
- 🐾 1 courgette (zucchini), grated
- 🐾 1 carrot, grated
- 🐾 A few lettuce leaves, finely shredded
- 🐾 2 salmon fillets

Makes
1
large pot

1. Bring the water to the boil in a medium-sized pan over a high heat. Add the vegetables and give everything a good stir. Place the salmon fillets on top of the vegetables. Cover the pan with a lid, reduce the heat to medium and poach the salmon for 10 minutes until it is cooked through and the vegetables are soft.

2. When it is cool enough to handle, break up the salmon into chunks, making sure there are no stray bones. If you have used salmon fillets with the skin on, cut the skin into small pieces and return it to the pan with the fish.

63

Tip You can add a few peeled prawns (shrimp) and/or shelled mussels to this, too, if you want to be particularly fancy.

Daily grind

Unlike humans, cats don't really chew their food. They use their teeth to tear at their prey and their little rough tongues like rasps to get the meat off the bone, and then they often swallow the pieces whole. Their jaws don't really move from side to side, but the strong down bite makes it easier to hold onto their prey.

Make it fast!

I've been cooking for my cat and my dogs using a pressure cooker for a few years now, and I can't believe it took me so long to discover the near-miracle of this piece of equipment, which can transform the cheapest, toughest cuts of meat into melting tenderness in half an hour or so. It means I can make a month's worth of meals for the freezer in just a couple of hours.

I suppose pressure cookers used to give me the fear because they reminded me of the ancient one that used to scream rather terrifyingly on my grandmother's stove when I was growing up. I was quite certain it was going to explode and take the roof off. Of course, it never did. Then a friend, food writer Catherine Phipps, wrote an excellent book, *The Pressure Cooker Cookbook: 150 Simple, Essential, Time-Saving Recipes*, and I instantly became a convert. I use it when I am cooking for humans, obviously, but it's a great time-saver when I'm cooking for my animals too. If you're a bit timid about giving it a go, I'd encourage you to try one out – a basic one is fairly inexpensive and will do the job perfectly, and you can always find near-new used ones on eBay.

Freeze!

I freeze my one-pot meals in portion sizes, and then just defrost them in the refrigerator the night before I want to give them to Dixie. Sometimes I warm them up slightly too, as that makes them so much more delicious. I also freeze the components of meals in portion sizes, so I can throw things together at the last minute: cooked millet (see page 41); brown rice; leftover cooked meat such as chicken, duck, beef or lamb; stock in ice-cube trays so it defrosts quickly. It transforms the freezer drawer into quite the feline deli counter.

Love your leftovers

I firmly believe in not throwing out a scrap of food if I can possibly help it, and I definitely use leftover human food in Dixie's dinners wherever I can. There are a couple of things to bear in mind, though. I use simply roasted meats and fish which haven't been cooked with onions or garlic, and have no wine in the gravy or sauce. I also cut off any extra fat. If I am making stock, I often make a basic stock without any salt or garlic (see page 38) and ladle out some for Dixie, before tossing in more seasonings and letting it cook longer for our own human consumption. I suppose this is more planned-overs than leftovers, but it's a great time saver.

THE TUNA CONUNDRUM

Have you ever paused to make a tuna sandwich for your lunch only to have your cat come racing from the far corners of the house to join you? Yep. Been there. I've never met a cat who didn't love tuna – it's like kitty crack. Every now and again, it's fine to indulge their habit but it should be a rare treat (I sometimes use a few flakes almost like a condiment on another, healthier meal, if Dixie is off her food – see page 100).

The problem with tuna is that they love its strong taste and smell so much that they will devour it to the exclusion of other foods. It is not a complete food and if your cat is hooked on tuna, she runs a very real chance of malnutrition. It is lacking in Vitamin E, which can lead to steatitis, a.k.a. the delightfully named Yellow Fat Disease. This, and its lack of other essential vitamins, can weaken your cat's immunity. So back off, kitty – keep that sandwich for yourself.

SUPPLEMENTARY QUESTIONS

Salmon oil can be a healthy addition to your cat's diet. It's a good source of Omega 3 fatty acids, which cannot be made by the body and need to be ingested. It can improve cat's skin, coat, joints and circulation as well as boosting the immune system. Buy high-quality, pet-grade oil and build up gradually, starting by sprinkling a single drop or two on your cat's dinner. They shouldn't have more than one teaspoon a day. Do consult your vet if you would like to learn more.

Plaque Off (see Resources, page 108) is a powdered seaweed I feed to both my dogs and my cat. It helps to combat plaque build-up, which can lead to tartar, and bad breath. It comes with a tiny spoon to sprinkle the supplement over their food, which I do twice a day. A word of caution, though: it should not be given to cats who are receiving treatment for hyperthyroidism, so check with your vet if necessary.

HOW TO MAKE AN
INDOOR KITTY GARDEN

If your cat is an indoor cat, or it's winter and she's less keen to go outside, or just because it's pretty and it would give her so much pleasure, it's a very nice idea to fill a few sturdy, difficult-to-knock-over planters with some safe-to-nibble plants.

🐾 **Catgrass** is usually a combination of barley, oats, wheat and rye. Nibbling on it is a behavioural instinct – it helps digestion and aids in expelling fur balls. My Cat Grass (see Resources, page 108) supplies seeds, grow-your-own kits, or live plants, either as a one-off or as a subscription service so you receive some every month or so.

🐾 Most people know how much cats love **catnip**. It can make them sleepy, or it can drive them crazy – you never know until they try it. Kittens seldom react to it until they reach about six months old, and some cats are quite indifferent to it. I have a hard time keeping this as an indoor plant as Dixie will chew it right down to the stem, but you might have better luck than me.

🐾 A planter of **herbs** not only smells delicious, it will delight your cat too. Try mint, rosemary or cat thyme *(Teucrium marum)*, alone or in combination.

• •

WHAT TO AVOID

Some common houseplants are very toxic to cats. All parts of lilies are poisonous, right down to the pollen, so avoid having them in your house, either potted or in a vase. A few specks of pollen which might drop onto their fur which they then lick off while grooming themselves can be fatal, so best not to let them into the house at all. Other common houseplants to avoid are peace lilies, philodendrons, amaryllis, cyclamen, azaleas and tulips, but this is by no means an exhaustive list, so do check before you bring plants into your cat's home.

HOW TO MAKE A
CATNIP MOUSE

This is a simple, fun project which doesn't require any special sewing
skills and is a great way to use up small scraps of fabric. Even quite
small children seem to enjoy experimenting with different colours and
textures to create these little mice, so do rope them in too. They make
charming gifts for other cat owners, too (see pages 94–5).

- Piece of paper, for template
- Some scraps of strong cotton fabric, corduroy or tweed
- String or ribbon for the tails
- Pins
- Needle and thread
- Hollow fibre toy stuffing, available from craft suppliers
- 2 tsp dried catnip (you can buy this online if you don't grow your own)
- Scraps of felt for the ears
- Embroidery floss for the eyes

1. Draw a symmetrical heart-shaped template on the paper, with the heart approximately 20cm/8in at its widest point. Cut out the heart template, pin to your fabric and cut around it. Cut the fabric in half vertically so that you have two matching pieces.

2. Place the right sides of the fabric together. Tuck the tail into position, with the main length of the tail sandwiched between the fabric so that you catch it as you sew around the mouse. Pin together and stitch, leaving a gap of 2.5cm/1in in the base of the mouse - you can do this on a sewing machine, although you can probably handstitch it with a needle and thread in the time it would take you to get the sewing machine out. Turn the mouse the right side out and press.

3. Fill the mouse with the hollow fibre and the catnip, then sew up the gap in the seam. Cut small triangles of felt for the ears and stitch them securely in place. Embroider small crosses for eyes.

'Way down deep, we're all motivated by the same urges. Cats have the courage to live by them.'

Jim Davis, Garfield cartoonist

Chapter Four

TREATS AND SPECIAL OCCASIONS

Cats bring so much pleasure to our lives, so sometimes they deserve something special in return. I know we have been talking about how their diets should comprise mostly meat, but the occasional special treat won't do any harm. They help with bonding, make tempting rewards, and the whiff of them can often bring a reluctant cat in from the garden.

SALMON AND SWEET POTATO CRUNCHIES

These make a good little snack and are very easy to throw together. I keep ice-cube trays full of puréed vegetables in the freezer so I don't have to fiddle about making up such small quantities every time I want to bake some treats.

- 🐾 213-g/7-oz can of salmon with no added salt, drained
- 🐾 80g/3oz/¼ cup puréed sweet potato
- 🐾 1 tsp finely chopped fresh mint or catnip
- 🐾 250g/9oz/2 cups brown rice flour, plus more for dusting

Tip Most of the recipes in this chapter make a lot of treats in one go. You can bake and then freeze them, or wrap the uncooked dough in small batches and freeze for up to 4 months. That way you can bake a small batch of treats whenever you need them.

Makes *Loads*

1. Preheat the oven to 180°C/Fan 160°C/350°F/Gas 4. Line a couple of baking sheets with parchment paper.

2. Pulse the drained salmon, sweet potato and mint together in a food processor until well combined. Add the flour and pulse until it forms a stiff dough - if it's still a little sticky, add a bit more flour until it's dry enough to roll out.

3. Roll out the dough on a surface lightly dusted with flour until it's about 6mm/ ¼ in thick. Using a sharp knife or a pizza cutter wheel, cut the dough into 1-cm/ ½-in squares.

4. Arrange on the prepared sheets (you might have to do this in two batches, depending on the size of your baking sheets and oven). Bake in the preheated oven for 25 minutes or until lightly browned. Remove from the oven and leave to cool and dry out on the sheets.

5. Once completely cool, these will keep in a sealed jar for 10 days, or you can freeze them for up to 4 months.

VARIATION

You can make these with canned tuna (in spring water), too (but see page 66).

CHICKEN AND SPINACH OATMEAL COOKIES

🐾 200g/7oz/1½ cups cooked chicken,
   very finely chopped

🐾 100g/3½oz/1 cup rolled oats (oatmeal)

🐾 50g/1¾oz/¼ cup cooked spinach,
   excess water squeezed out

🐾 1 egg, lightly beaten

Makes
30
approx.

Who doesn't love a cookie? These are a tasty treat, perfect for using up any leftover roast chicken you might have.

· ● · · · · ● · · ● · · · ● ● · · ● · · ● · · ● · · ● · ● · · ● · · ● · · ● ● · · · ● ● · ●

1. Preheat the oven to 200°C/Fan 180°C/400°F/Gas 6. Line a baking sheet with parchment paper.

2. In a bowl, mix together all the ingredients until everything is very well combined. Drop teaspoons of the mixture onto the parchment paper, leaving some space between each one, as they will spread out a little. Press with the back of a spoon to flatten them out a bit.

3. Bake in the preheated oven for about 20 minutes until cooked through. Leave on the baking sheet to cool before serving to your cat. These will keep in the refrigerator for a couple of days or in the freezer for 4 months.

SARDINE SNACKIES

Wheat isn't very easily digestible for many cats, so blitzing up more palatable rolled oats (oatmeal) in a food processor until very fine makes a good substitute for wheat flour.

- 🐾 120g/4¹/₂oz/1¹/₃ cups rolled oats (oatmeal)
- 🐾 120-g/4¹/₂-oz can of sardines, drained and blotted of excess oil
- 🐾 3 tbsp finely chopped fresh parsley
- 🐾 Flour, for dusting

Makes
Loads

1. Preheat the oven to 180°C/Fan 160°C/350°F/Gas 4. Line a couple of baking sheets with parchment paper.

2. In a food processor, blitz the oats (oatmeal) until fine, like a coarse flour. Add the drained sardines and parsley and pulse into a firm dough. If the dough is very stiff, add some water, a teaspoon at a time and pulsing after each addition, until you have the right consistency.

3. Turn the dough onto a lightly floured surface and roll it out until it is about 6mm/¼in thick. Using a sharp knife or a pizza cutter wheel, cut the dough into 1-cm/½-in squares.

4. Arrange on the prepared sheets (you might have to do this in two batches, depending on the size of your baking sheets and oven). Bake in the preheated oven for about 20 minutes or until lightly browned. Remove from the oven and leave to cool and dry out on the sheets.

5. Once completely cool, these will keep in a sealed jar in the refrigerator for 7 days, or you can freeze them for up to 4 months.

VARIATION
You can make this with canned pilchards (in oil, not tomato sauce) or mackerel too.

SQUASHY
LIVER TREATS

These aren't going to win any best-in-show beauty contests, but Dixie loves them. Though excessive consumption of liver can lead to a vitamin A toxicity, devouring it as an occasional treat is fine. If you share your house with dogs as well as cats, you'll find that dogs enjoy these too.

- 🐾 200g/7oz chicken livers
- 🐾 80g/3oz/½ cup cooked, puréed butternut squash
- 🐾 1 egg
- 🐾 250g/9oz/2 cups brown rice flour, plus more for dusting

Makes
Loads

1. Preheat the oven to 180°C/Fan 160°C/350°F/Gas 4. Line a couple of baking sheets with parchment paper.

2. Pour about 200ml/7fl oz/³⁄₄ cup water into a pan and bring to the boil. Add the chicken livers to the water and boil gently for about 5 minutes until they are completely cooked through with no hint of pink. Drain and place in a food processor with the butternut squash and the egg. Process until very smooth, then add the rice flour. Pulse until well combined.

3. Turn the dough out onto a lightly floured surface and roll it out until it is about 6mm/¹⁄₄in thick. Using a sharp knife or a pizza cutter wheel, cut the dough into 1-cm/¹⁄₂-in squares.

4. Arrange on the prepared sheets (you might have to do this in two batches, depending on the size of your baking sheets and oven). Bake in the preheated oven for about 25–28 minutes until lightly browned. Remove from the oven and leave to cool and dry out on the sheets.

5. Once completely cool, these will keep in a sealed jar in the refrigerator for a couple of days, or you can freeze them for up to 4 months.

MINI HAMBURGERS

- 500g/1lb 2oz minced (ground) beef, 5% fat
- 100g/3½oz/½ cup cooked spinach, excess water squeezed out
- 1 tsp chopped fresh thyme leaves

Makes
30
approx.

These are always popular. You can switch the beef for other kinds of minced (ground) meat, and the spinach for squash or sweet potato if you like.

• •

1. Preheat the oven to 200°C/Fan 180°C/400°F/Gas 6. Line a roasting pan with parchment paper.

2. In a bowl, mix together all the ingredients with your hands until everything is very well combined. Break off walnut-sized pieces and roll them into balls, then flatten into patty shapes and place in the prepared pan.

3. Bake in the preheated oven for 18-22 minutes, until entirely cooked through. These will keep sealed in the refrigerator for a couple of days, or freeze for up to 4 months.

PRAWN CRACKERS

This is definitely a favourite snack with, Dixie, who is quite
the princess.

- 200g/7oz/1½ cups cooked, peeled prawns (shrimp)
- 150g/5½oz/1½ cups rolled oats (oatmeal)
- 3 tbsp finely chopped fresh parsley
- 1 tsp olive oil
- Flour, for dusting

Makes
Loads

1. Place all the ingredients in a food processor and blitz until they form a smooth paste. Chill in the refrigerator for 20-30 minutes.

2. Preheat the oven to 200°C/Fan 180°C/400°F/Gas 6. Line a baking sheet with parchment paper.

3. This is quite a sticky dough, so it's easier to roll it out between two pieces of parchment paper. Lightly dust the bottom piece of parchment paper with flour, then roll out the dough under the second piece of parchment until it is 6mm/¼in thick. Dip a 2-cm/¾-in cutter into some flour (if you don't have a small cutter, a bottle cap will do) and cut the dough into circles. Place the circles on the baking sheet, then gather up the scraps of dough, knead together and roll out and continue to cut out circles until you have used up all of the dough.

4. Bake in the preheated oven for about 18-20 minutes until lightly browned. Remove from the oven and leave to cool and dry out on the sheets.

5. Once completely cool, these will keep in a sealed jar in the refrigerator for a couple of days, or you can freeze them for up to 4 months.

REMEMBER

How much you feed your cat depends on her size, age, weight and how active she is (see page 16).

BIRTHDAY CAKE MUFFINS

....

These are a great way to celebrate your cat's birthday or any other special occasion. If you make them in a normal-sized muffin pan, you will need to feed your cat this special treat a bit at a time, or use a mini-muffin pan for a perfectly cat-sized snack.

For the muffins

- 🐾 1 tsp olive oil
- 🐾 500g/1lb 2oz minced (ground) beef, lamb or turkey
- 🐾 225g/8oz/1 cup mashed sweet potato
- 🐾 1 egg, lightly beaten
- 🐾 2 tsp chopped fresh catnip or 1 tsp dried catnip

To finish

- 🐾 2 tbsp plain live yogurt (see page 29)
- 🐾 A little more catnip, to garnish

Makes
12
muffins or 24 mini muffins

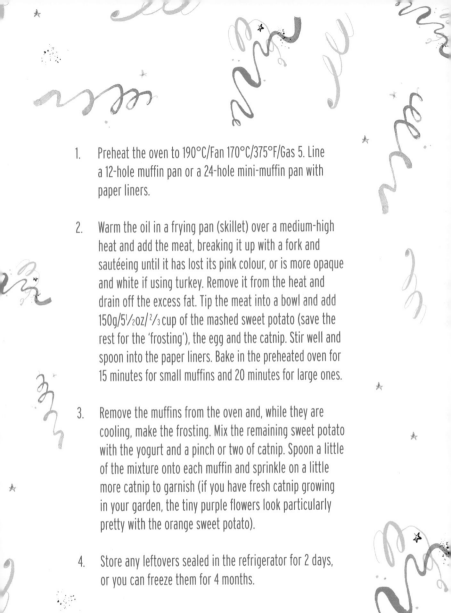

1. Preheat the oven to 190°C/Fan 170°C/375°F/Gas 5. Line a 12-hole muffin pan or a 24-hole mini-muffin pan with paper liners.

2. Warm the oil in a frying pan (skillet) over a medium-high heat and add the meat, breaking it up with a fork and sautéeing until it has lost its pink colour, or is more opaque and white if using turkey. Remove it from the heat and drain off the excess fat. Tip the meat into a bowl and add 150g/5¹/₂oz/²/₃ cup of the mashed sweet potato (save the rest for the 'frosting'), the egg and the catnip. Stir well and spoon into the paper liners. Bake in the preheated oven for 15 minutes for small muffins and 20 minutes for large ones.

3. Remove the muffins from the oven and, while they are cooling, make the frosting. Mix the remaining sweet potato with the yogurt and a pinch or two of catnip. Spoon a little of the mixture onto each muffin and sprinkle on a little more catnip to garnish (if you have fresh catnip growing in your garden, the tiny purple flowers look particularly pretty with the orange sweet potato).

4. Store any leftovers sealed in the refrigerator for 2 days, or you can freeze them for 4 months.

CATSICLES

🐾 Cooked chicken or beef, drained canned salmon or poached fish (be careful to remove any bones)

🐾 Salt-free chicken stock, broth from the Chicken Soup (see page 38), or water

🐾 A few dry treats (optional)

Makes quite a few

These are cool snacks for hot days. Of course, when the temperature rises you should make sure your cat always has a plentiful supply of fresh water, but these make a great chilly treat when you want to give him something a little more exciting. Devouring them exercises his brain too, which is never a bad thing.

• •

1. Put the meat or fish in a blender or food processor with a good slosh of chicken stock or water. Process until very smooth. You may want to add a little more liquid at this point, depending on the texture you're after.

2. Stir in a few dried treats if you like, for extra texture and interest. Spoon into ice-cube trays and freeze. Your cat will love to lick and nibble on these on swelteringly hot days.

Using a
DEHYDRATOR
TO MAKE EASY, HEALTHY TREATS

When I wrote my previous book, I discovered the joys of using a dehydrator to make healthy dog snacks. You don't need a fancy one and mine is now working double time, as I use it to make snacks for my dogs, Barney and Gracie, and for my cat, Dixie, too.

They are fun to experiment with - try drying out any of the biscuit or cracker recipes instead of cooking them. And they are great for drying out small pieces of fruit, such as blueberries or slices of apple. Your cat may not be too interested in them, but you might enjoy them yourself.

'I love cats because I enjoy my home; and little by little they become its invisible soul.'

Jean Cocteau

Chicken livers

Cleaned and halved, these make a very good dehydrated snack. Dry them for 4-8 hours, until they are completely dried out when you cut through them.

Salmon bites

Pulse together a drained can of salmon with 2-3 tbsp finely chopped catnip or cat grass (see Resources, page 108), 2 tbsp rolled oats (oatmeal) and 1 tsp plain yogurt (see page 29) in a food processor until it has the texture of a coarse paste. Break into marble-sized pieces, flatten slightly and dry for 9-10 hours.

Prawns (shrimp)

Leave whole and dry them for 4-8 hours, until they are completely dried out when you cut through them.

Tuna treats

Just break the drained tuna into chunks and dry for 9-10 hours (see The Tuna Conundrum, page 66).

Meat jerky

Cut skinless, boneless chicken, duck, venison or beef into thin strips, along the grain of the meat. Leave the strips to dry for 4-12 hours, until each piece is a uniform colour and completely dried out when you cut through it. Snip into bite-sized pieces with scissors.

CAN YOU TRAIN A CAT?

• •

First of all, forget all thoughts of dogs. They evolved to create highly complex, interdependent working relationships with humans while cats were off on their own catching mice. It's a little more complex to get cats to do your bidding, but it is entirely possible. I first became aware that cats were trainable when I lived in Russia for a couple of years. Most people lived in small, crowded apartments, often with no outside space. If you're sharing a small space, litter trays aren't ideal. So what did people do? They trained their cats to use the loo, teaching them to perch on the edge of the seat to do their business. If you can train a cat to do that, you can certainly train one to come when called, sit, or do a high five.

It's important to start slowly and not to expect too much too quickly. Begin by setting aside five minutes a couple of times a day, and arm yourself with your cat's favourite treats. Decide on a special noise you will make only when you want to get your cat's attention, or buy a clicker. Position yourself within a few metres (yards) of the cat and make the noise or press the clicker. When she looks up, hold out her favourite treat. If she comes to you, give her the treat. Repeat this exercise, getting further and further away, until she begins to associate the noise with getting a treat and lots of fuss from you.

Once you have this cracked, you can teach her to sit when she comes to you by raising the treat directly above her head (not too high, as this will probably make her prance on her back feet). As soon as her bottom hits the floor, give her a treat and make the noise, so she associates the noise with pleasing you and getting something delicious to eat. If you enjoy this, you can waste (spend, sorry, spend) years of your life on YouTube, where there are thousands of cat training videos for your entertainment and edification.

The most important principle of cat training – as with dogs – is that you train them with positive reinforcement. Scolding a cat is a really good way of ensuring they will cease to entertain your nonsense and go and find something better to do.

If you have an indoor cat, this is a great way to exercise their bodies and minds. Also, if you have a timid cat, or a rescue cat who is new to your home, a little light training is a very good way of gently building up your bond.

CATIQUETTE
Teaching your cat some basic table manners

Try to deter your cat from climbing up on the kitchen table, or onto the counter tops. It's not very hygienic for you, and it is potentially dangerous for her, as she may get into foods not meant for her or skirt dangerously close to hot pans and boiling liquids. One of the best ways to encourage good behaviour is to ensure no one in the household, guests included, ever feeds the cat titbits from the table. A more drastic way is to place empty, washed food cans filled with some small coins or pebbles right on the edge of the counter tops. Cats hate loud, sudden noises and the shock of knocking one of the cans and it clattering onto the floor is sometimes enough to deter them.

Presents for cat friends

'Nobody who is not prepared to spoil cats will get from them the reward they are able to give to those who do spoil them.'

Compton Mackenzie

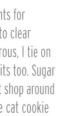

Any of the biscuit treats in this chapter make great presents for friends who have cats. I make up batches and put them into clear cellophane bags tied with ribbon and, if I am feeling generous, I tie on a cat-shaped cookie cutter for them to make human biscuits too. Sugar Shack (see Resources, page 108) has a great selection, but shop around on Etsy and Amazon, especially around Halloween when the cat cookie cutter business seems to go into overdrive. I sometimes make up the cat treats in fancy shapes if I am giving them as a gift as they look so much prettier, but it's probably a good idea to break them into small pieces before you feed them to a cat.

Put a pinch or two of dried catnip in a paper bag and scrunch it up into a ball.

Place a few small pebbles or little bells in a plastic drinks bottle, put the top back on and let your cat roll it about the floor. Alternatively, put some treats inside and leave the top off – your cat will have fun trying to wriggle the treats out.

The happy indoor cat

Keeping an indoor cat happy takes a little more effort on your part than with a free-to-roam feline. You need to pay particular attention to keeping his litter tray clean (see page 20) and set aside time to actively play with him each day. Provide them with plenty of opportunities to pounce and fulfil their prey-hunting instincts - give them fishing pole toys (see page 30), catnip mice (see page 70), and little balls to chase. A bed on a shelf near a window, particularly if you set up a bird feeder outside, is like giving them a lifetime subscription to Netflix. Plenty of different scratching posts (see page 46) around your home help too, particularly if they are of different heights with platforms for the cat to perch on.

The cardboard tube from a loo roll makes a great toy if you fill it with a few treats. Fold the ends together to seal roughly - you still need a small gap so the treats can escape when the cat rolls the tube around and paws at it.

Tie a small soft toy securely with a length of ribbon and tie the other end to a banister or a door handle, so it is suspended about 30cm/12in above the ground.

HOW TO MAKE A
CARDBOARD
CAT PLAYHOUSE

All cats love to have places where they can hide away and gather their thoughts. Making a playhouse from cardboard boxes is a fun project, particularly if you get children involved. This can be a minimalist haven, or embellished with all manner of patterns and extravagant detail, depending on your own personal taste.

- A cutting board or newspapers
- Metal ruler
- Craft knife
- 1 large, sturdy cardboard box
- A sheet of cardboard to make the roof - this could come from another cardboard box
- Dinner and tea plates, to use as templates
- Glue gun and glue, or strong craft glue - I like pet-safe Gorilla Glue
- Paint and paintbrushes
- A blanket and/or pillow to put inside the playhouse

1. If you don't have a cutting board, use layers of newspaper to protect the surface you're working on from the craft knife.

2. Using the metal ruler and craft knife, carefully cut the flaps from the longest sides of the top of the box. Next, cut the remaining short sides into triangles to help form the pointed roof. Cut some strips of cardboard and glue them to the inside of the box as supports to help keep the pointed flaps upright.

3. Using a plate as a template (I like to use two different sizes of plate), draw some round window openings around the box. Draw an entrance hole at the base of the box. Carefully cut them out using the craft knife.

4. Cut the second piece of cardboard into a sheet large enough to cover the box with about 10cm/4in extra all around to create an overhang on the roof. Fold it firmly in half along the middle and use your glue gun or craft glue to secure the roof to the box. Leave to dry.

5. Next comes the fun part - paint and decorate the box as you wish. Let it dry completely. To finish, place a blanket and a pillow inside the house to guarantee your cat's enduring affection.

Chapter Five

FEEL-BETTER FOOD

When our beloved feline companions
are ailing or elderly, suffering from allergies
or just simply off their food for a while, we
all want to do as much as we can to get them
healthy and keep them happy. Of course,
food can help, but if your cat has unusual or
persistent symptoms it is vital you seek your
vet's advice immediately.

FASTING

By nature cats are frequent mini-fasters – in their pre-domesticated state, they would not eat for hours at a time. So don't worry if your cat has a day when she's off her food. All sorts of things can upset them and make them reluctant to eat; as long as they are still drinking water they should be fine. If this persists for more than a day or so though, do call your vet.

TEMPTATION

If your cat is reluctant to eat, warming her food slightly, pouring a little warmed, salt-free stock over the top, or sprinkling on a small amount of delicious, smelly tuna see (The Tuna Conundrum, page 66) can help to reactivate her appetite. Sometimes very gentle dishes like simple chicken soup (see page 38), or just some warm, diluted salt-free stock on its own is nutritious and can tide cats over for a day or so until their appetites return.

UNDER-THE-WEATHER FOOD

When Dixie is sick, I follow the Blue Cross (see Resources, page 108) guidelines for taking care of her. All cats have occasional bouts of vomiting (sometimes it's just something as simple as expelling a furball) and diarrhoea. If it seems more serious than that and has gone on for more than 24 hours, of course I call my vet. In the meantime, I don't feed her for 12 hours after the vomiting has stopped and keep her inside where I can keep an eye on her. Then I begin by feeding her tiny amounts – just a teaspoon or two – of poached chicken or white fish. If she keeps that down, I give her a little more a couple of hours later and gradually over the following couple of days, I reintroduce more of her normal food alongside the bland diet.

FOOD FOR SORE MOUTHS

As cats get older, or after any kind of dental treatment, they often have sore mouths, missing teeth and painful gums. Cats manage quite well with few or even no teeth. They don't chew their food as we do (see page 64), so it's fine within reason if they gulp it down. To minimize any pain, you should purée their food in a food processor or with a stick blender. You can feed them exclusively cooked meat or fish, or add about 10 per cent cooked vegetables to this poorly-mouth diet.

🐾 **Some cooked meat and fish suggestions:** chicken, chicken livers, lamb, canned pilchards or sardines (packed in oil, with the excess oil blotted off on kitchen paper), poached white fish or salmon.

🐾 **Some cooked vegetable ideas:** broccoli, carrots, peas, squash, sweet potato.

Tip

Gums are a good indicator of your cat's health. They should be nice and pink and smooth. If they are red and swollen, this is a sign there might be a dental problem. If they're pale for more than a couple of days, this can indicate that your cat is unwell and you should call your vet.

DEALING WITH ALLERGIES AND INTOLERANCES

Allergies happen when your cat's immune system reacts strongly to foods and other everyday substances found in her environment. Symptoms that indicate your cat might have allergies include:

- Sneezing or wheezing
- Watery and itchy eyes
- Itchy skin
- Runny nose
- Irritated ears and frequent ear infections
- Excessive scratching
- Vomiting
- Diarrhoea

If you think your cat has allergies, discuss it with your vet who will probably advise skin sensitivity tests and possibly an elimination diet over the course of a few weeks, after which you slowly reintroduce into his diet his usual foods to see which ones he is reacting to.

As well as foods, cats can be allergic to dust and fleas. Prevention is the best policy here. If you think she has a dust allergy, use a dust-free, unscented litter, wash her bedding frequently and embark on a vigorous vacuuming routine (sorry!) With fleas, use de-fleaing medication prescribed by your vet. The ones you commonly find in pet shops can be actively harmful to some cats, so are best avoided.

IS YOUR CAT CHEWING MORE THAN HER DINNER?

If your cat is chewing on the furniture, or scratching at it, it's a good idea to try to nip this behaviour in the bud before it gets too deeply ingrained. Sticking double-sided tape over fabric she is trying to shred, or covering it in kitchen foil (this sometimes works for counter tops and tables you don't want her to walk on, too) can work if you are consistent in applying it over a period of weeks. It's also a good idea to provide several scratching posts (see page 46) so she can stretch her spine and condition her claws without wrecking the joint.

You can also buy sprays, such as bitter apple spray, which help to deter bad habits. Alternatively, you can safely make your own, using a spray bottle bought from a garden centre or homeware store (never reuse a spray bottle that has had cleaning fluids or similar in it). When you make up your spray, test it on an inconspicuous corner of the fabric or surface you would like to treat first, just to make sure it doesn't damage any special finishes.

1. Bottle up a mixture of one part cider vinegar and one part water. To the human nose, the vinegar smell soon dissipates, but cats' sense of smell is 14 times stronger than humans' so it remains off-putting to them for quite a long time.

2. Mix together about 200ml/7fl oz/¾ cup water with 25 drops of essential oils such as citronella, lemon or orange. There is some new research about cats and lavender oil, which indicates it may be harmful. It's inconclusive, but probably it's better to leave it out just in case. Add a tiny splash of vodka (cheers!) or a single drop of dishwashing liquid to help disperse the oils and give it a good shake before using it.

HOW TO MAKE A
CAT PILLOW

This is so easy and you can even hand stitch it if you don't have a sewing machine. Use sturdy material on one side and fur fabric on the other, or just use the same fabric for the whole thing. Whatever you choose, make sure it's a washable fabric so you can toss it into the washing machine when you need to.

'Cats are connoisseurs of comfort.'

James Herriot

. . . .

🐾 1 piece of sturdy fabric, such as denim or heavy cotton, about 60-cm/24-in square

🐾 1 piece of fur fabric, about 60-cm/24-in square

🐾 Hollow fibre toy stuffing

🐾 Scissors

🐾 Pins, needles, thread

🐾 Embroidery floss

1. Lay the fabric on a flat surface, right sides together, and pin all the way around the edges. Stitch together, about 2cm/³⁄₄in from the edges, making sure you leave a 15-cm/6-in gap in one side.

2. Turn the pillow cover right sides out and fill with the stuffing. Stitch the gap closed. Fluff the pillow so that the filling is evenly distributed. Use the embroidery floss to make several stitches in the middle of the pillow, ensuring you go right through both layers of fabric. Fasten off the floss. This makes a nice hollow for your cat to sit in and helps to stop the filling moving around too much.

. . . .

VARIATION

I made a patchwork pillow for Dixie using several pairs of old jeans which I cut up into 20-cm/8-in squares. I stitched the back pocket from one of the pairs to one of the sides of the pillow before sewing everything together. Then I made some small muslin sachets of dried catnip, camomile and valerian which I tucked into the pocket to make the pillow more interesting for her. You can make up a lot of sachets at once and seal the ones you're not using in a ziplock bag in the freezer until you need them – they don't lose any of their smelly potency that way.

RESOURCES

CRAFT MATERIALS
Nutshell Natural Paints / Green Building Supply
Low-odour, non-toxic paints in a wide range of colours, suitable for craft projects.
nutshellpaints.co.uk
greenbuildingsupply.com

Ropelocker / Screwfix / Home Depot
For items mentioned in the scratching post project.
ropelocker.co.uk
screwfix.com
homedepot.com

FOOD AND SUPPLEMENTS
Lily's Kitchen
High-quality, complete dry and wet cat food.
lilyskitchen.co.uk

My Cat Grass / PetCo
Fresh cat grass and seeds.
mycatgrass.co.uk
petco.com

Natural Instinct / Nature's Menu
Complete, raw, frozen cat food. Nature's Menu also does dry and wet cat food.
naturalinstinct.com
naturesmenu.co.uk

Plaque Off / Sweden Care USA
For Plaque Off Powder Cat dental supplement.
plaqueoff.com
swedencareusa.com

KITCHEN APPLIANCES
Appliances Direct / Argos / Lakeland
For a good range of dehydrators, blenders, pressure cookers and general cookery equipment.
appliancesdirect.co.uk
argos.co.uk
lakeland.co.uk

Sugar Shack / Wilton
For animal-shaped cookie cutters.
sugarshack.co.uk
wilton.com

Williams Sonoma
For durable kitchen tools, including immersion blenders and baking supplies.
williams-sonoma.com

CAT CARE ADVICE
Blue Cross / PetMd
Useful resources on cat care advice. Consult your vet immediately about any serious concerns.
bluecross.org.uk
petmd.com

ACKNOWLEDGEMENTS

Thank you so much to all of the Pavilion gang, for their cheerfulness, humour, patience and professionalism in making this the book it is. Polly Powell, Katie Cowan, Bella Cockrell, Helen Lewis, and Michelle Mac, you are all a joy to work with and I am enormously grateful to have had you on my side while coaxing this project into life.

I continue to be surprised and enchanted by Cinzia Zenocchini's enormous talent as an artist and I feel hugely fortunate that she has provided the illustrations for this book.

A massive thank you to Caroline Michel and Tessa David at Peters Fraser & Dunlop for excellent advice and hand-holding always.

Séan Donnellan, you rock and no one does a midnight *mise en place* better than you. Thank you for the recipe testing, as well as absolutely everything else, always.

And my eternal gratitude to Delphi, Liberty, Oscar, Prune and Dixie, all of the cats I have loved, who have taught me a lifetime's worth of lessons in living in the moment and extracting every drop of pleasure from every single day, even when that includes sitting on the keyboard.

ABOUT THE AUTHOR

Debora Robertson is a food, gardening and lifestyle writer and editor. She has written for a wide variety of publications, including the *Guardian*, the *Daily Telegraph*, the *Sunday Telegraph*, *The Times*, the *Sunday Times*, the *Daily Mail*, *Country Life* and *Delicious* magazine. She lives in London with her husband Séan, her dogs, Barney and Gracie, and her very grand cat, Dixie. Her previous book *Dogs' Dinners* is also published by Pavilion.

INDEX